GIANT
PANDAS

by Trudi Strain Trueit

AMICUS HIGH INTEREST AMICUS INK

Amicus High Interest and Amicus Ink
are imprints of Amicus
P.O. Box 1329, Mankato, MN 56002
www.amicuspublishing.us

Library of Congress Cataloging-in-Publication Data

Trueit, Trudi Strain, author.
  Giant pandas / Trudi Strain Trueit.
      pages cm. -- (Wild bears)
  "Amicus High Interest is published by Amicus."
  Summary: "Presents information about rare giant pandas, their habitats
in China, and their diet of bamboo."-- Provided by publisher.
  Audience: K to grade 3.
  Includes bibliographical references and index.
  ISBN 978-1-60753-774-8 (library binding)
  ISBN 978-1-60753-873-8 (ebook)
  ISBN 978-1-68152-025-4 (paperback)
  1. Giant panda--Juvenile literature. I. Title.
  QL737.C27T774 2015
  599.789--dc23
                            2014043599

Photo Credits: ex0rzist/Shutterstock Images, cover; irakite/Shutterstock
Images, 2, 6–7; BIHAIBO/iStockphoto, 5, 22; Minden Pictures/SuperStock,
9, 16–17, 18; df028/Shutterstock Images, 10–11, 23; Fuse/Thinkstock,
13; View Stock/Stock Connection/Glow Images, 14; Hung Chung Chih/
iStockphoto, 21

Produced for Amicus by The Peterson Publishing Company
and Red Line Editorial.

Designer Becky Daum
Printed in Malaysia

HC 10 9 8 7 6 5 4 3 2 1
PB 10 9 8 7 6 5 4 3 2 1

TABLE OF CONTENTS

GIANT PANDA HABITATS

Giant pandas live in China.

Mountain **forests** are their homes.

These **habitats** are cool and rainy.

The forests are filled with **bamboo**.

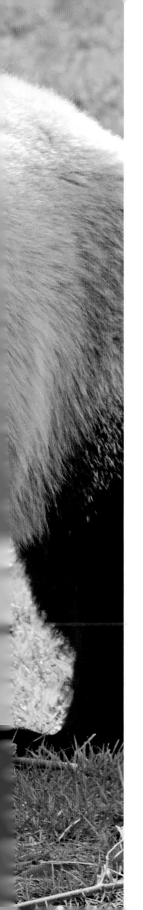

SPECIAL COLORS

Giant pandas have black and white fur. Black fur is around their eyes. Their ears and legs are also black.

PANDA SIZE

Giant pandas can weigh up to 275 pounds (125 kg). They are up to three feet (0.9 m) tall on all fours. They can stand up to six feet (1.8 m) tall on their back legs.

FAVORITE FOOD

Giant pandas eat bamboo. They grip it with their paws. Strong jaws help them chew. Their large teeth grind the bamboo.

Fun Fact
Pandas eat around 40 pounds (18 kg) of bamboo each day.

IN THE TREES

Giant pandas climb trees. Climbing keeps them safe from **predators**. Leopards hunt pandas on the forest floor.

LIVING ALONE

Giant pandas live alone. They brush their tails on the ground. This leaves a smell. It tells other pandas to stay away.

Fun Fact

Pandas growl at other pandas that come near.

STAYING WARM

Giant pandas sleep in logs or tree stumps. They climb down the mountains in winter. It is warmer at the bottom of the mountains.

RAISING CUBS

Giant pandas have one or two cubs each year. Cubs have all white hair when they are born. Black fur grows after a few weeks. Mothers raise cubs for about two years.

Fun Fact

Newborn pandas are the size of a stick of butter.

RARE BEARS

There are only about 1,600 giant pandas left in the wild. People have built **reserves** to help them. These habitats are protected. People give the bears plenty of bamboo to eat.

Fun Fact
China has more than 60 giant panda reserves.

GIANT PANDA FACTS

Size: 176–275 pounds (80–125 kg), 59–71 inches (1.5–1.8 m)

Range: China

Habitat: mountain forests

Number of babies: 1–2

Food: mainly bamboo; some other grasses and rodents